T0198804

Rowing to
RHODESIA

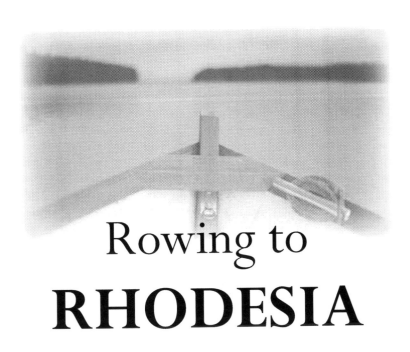

Rowing to
RHODESIA

JIM HINER

Order this book online at www.trafford.com
or email orders@trafford.com

Most Trafford titles are also available at major online book retailers.

Printed in the United States of America.

ISBN: 978-1-4669-5052-8 (hc)
ISBN: 978-1-4669-5050-4 (sc)
ISBN: 978-1-4669-5051-1 (e)

Library of Congress Control Number: 2012913800

Trafford rev. 07/31/2012

 www.trafford.com

North America & International
toll-free: 1 888 232 4444 (USA & Canada)
phone: 250 383 6864 ♦ fax: 812 355 4082

CONTENTS

DEDICATION

to *Connie* and *Tawn*, who caught the *newsreel* and *selected short subjects,*
    but had to leave early; and to
Maciej, who had to sit through the Main Feature twice.

THE BACK OF MY CALLING CARD

*

("If you can't write your idea on the back of my calling card, you don't have a clear idea."—David Belasco)

*

It was round and like a bowl
Spherical but also interrupted
Conversationally
With bronze or possibly
Cast iron, or even
Hammered tin or glint engraving
In the air with seven tongues
Obtrusive, and something like
On pipe, some flanges.

But equally
What might have crowned a king
Or, yes, a burly empress,
Of majestic presence
Not simply *one's perception.*

And yet the scientists said
Too suspended to be useful
Too complex to be informative
Too obfuscatory to be exclamatory
Too confound to be unladen like
A *quark*, a *nano*, or a *color*.

So neither physicists nor The Great
American Theatrical Producer
David Belasco
Could form a *clear idea*
Of why this icon was
But said that if it was
It was too uninterchangeable
To fit.

So *this* on you, Belasco,
Or Mister DesCartes, whatever
Your frenchy name.

So

much deepends me

from

wade to wallow

a mode much than

of

Performance:

what is all of

why.

ROWING TO RHODESIA
or:
"Poets Should Not Do *not*"

Poets should not do *not*
too much of the time
but poets should not
avoid it altogether.

So much depends
not upon now but on what
others have said before me on
obscurities of the specifics of
certain invisible faces of
even the most explicit
clearness of a word.
Or even of what they've not
said on such a word.

I come to a word now:
Byzantium. That is not
a word of what one would want
to go there, but of those
who only want to view
the domes, their *wows*
their golden boughs.

Before the full nether glory
of Sixth Century is specified
no specifics are palpable enough
to warrant a rush to the Ticket
Office. And the benefit
of certain monkey glands
can no further enticement
make and is a *not*. Void it,
the goyim woid. Avoid.

NEVER MENTION THE WORD

Never mention the word, you know,
what turns daylight crepuscular,
blind to the bone that's become
carnivorous. You don't see
what I mean still; so
never mention the word.

There are what we furthermore call
After-all words, after all
not renegade nor rare, you know,
nor float on gas. Words
not retrograde, no, but rather
memory-rested like a man
with his feet in the air at night
in an old barn or analog of lair.
Alas, we too seldom seek them out
from anchorage in the Wellingtons
and Waterloos of our mindsets,
these words that are to be preferred;
So prefer them.

They say, these some words say,
these after-all words: they should be
not saved for a ruinous day.
How atrocious to wait for the dangle
of all that might be precious
to hang from the corrupting shingle
of such a day!

Hardness, fact, meanwhile and
Totems of fact hold forth
and bimetallic arthroplasty
alone holds it all together where
those never-mention words appear.

But wait, be silent, hear
how providentially they will dissolve
dry up drown and disappear
while sweet ripe rich
darling buds of May
spray fragrance where
no mention ever is made.
So never make it.

I FEARED THAT NO ONE EVER WOULD ASK ME

I feared that no one ever would ask me
to tell the meaning of one of my poems
but then one recent metrical day
in a shrine of highly decorative means
I was asked exactly that, and was able
for five fine full hours to hold forth
at the start, and getting worked up some
spewed on (and on) for another thirty-six.

To be sure, the pay though a little more
than scale for busboys, was a little less
than I'd been led environmentally
to expect. Diagramming as much
to the Leader, I was explained to
with a flood of patient telluric charm
that the coffee was entirely on her
and couldn't I see that refills were free.

Well yes, true enough, but where was
the clamor, the crowding around,
and why aren't my elbows rubbed raw
like those of any even ordinary scoundrel?
And what of all those violent attempts
on one's body one's been led by all
the Byrons to expect? But I thanked her
for the plaque with my name on it in gilt.
Did I say "gilt"? Like gold, but in fiction,
what's audibly visible in poetic diction.

(Note: Here is a poem I wish I still liked; but I don't.)

CELEBRATION FOR DYLAN THOMAS' CRAFTY DEATH

Now your finally quiet bones will start pulsations
In some who paid no praise, nor merit Love;
But who suspicious now and now unconsummated
By what you called *tall nightingales and tears*,
Want quick illuminations to lighten fears
Of your sullen crafted art. They ask not love
But meanings plain in pages pure enough to flutter
In front of those who cannot see the moon, its rages.

How they'll tag you, now you're dead, *Discovered!*
And memorize your deeply buried bones—
No mystery left of what was expurgated.

So familiar will your name one day become,
Protesting worshippers will shake their dismal head
At other ash-collectors who pronounce you dead.

SO WHERE WAS I

So where was I when the stagnant smirch of doom
Settled upon us, all over the land lying on and under us,
Cringing whisperings among us, conspiratorially,
As we clanged our unredeemably boggy boots,
Embellishing all at our feet with the frays and fricassees
Of ancient wastes modernly occurring where effort
Soured and turned rancid in its turn, inhibitioning?

Think, think, think we thought, trusting ever
In all the Everlasting Amulets, gainsaying
Never no never, their owlish peekaboos with
Anachronistic nomenclatures.

Order was ordered; it was ambulatory:
We can *walk* with that, they said, as they fell into
Metaphysics of Euler's last theorem and squaring
Circles variously rendered as quite ordinarinesses.
(Grievances by the evermore, as E.A. Poe once certainly said.)

And there I was standing on some crag at Cornwall
Conspicuousing myelf posturingly; or was it
Some declivity at Dover, where all
The hypothetical Universe lapped hypothetically
At the beach, and the beach fought back
Exchanging loss for gain and taking sand
For sovereignty or for only serendipity,
Hoping the hole in the Universal Dike would stay
No greater than Brinker's thumb. *Fats,*
Meanwhile wallering out of patiently, asks,
"What *key* are you struggling in? Turn the page!"

That was at the *Sunset*, south side of Chicago
A time ago. A long ago. A long what-matter ago.

VERTICALITY

Sorrow and grandiloquence

On which we horizontal beings

Choke from dust of dead;

Poisonous airs arise

Stuffed at the spired feedlots

With self-inflationary hopes.

We take what comfort we can

On the level

Of posturepedic sand.

SCHOOLING

Standing before the broadcast world
Knowing not as much as a third grader
What Caesar's last words were:
I'll get you for this! Or that Chopin
Could play his mazurkas
As well with his toes as his fingers.

There is just constant amazement!
That Grigory Yefimovich
Rasputin, for example, reputedly
Used nothing but *Brut* after-shave
And a fifth grader knows as much as
A courtier a rascal a king or a mountebank.

The straws of knowledge of learning
Of schooling do not float do not alter
Disappear do not bind, synthesize
Alas not, nor make mind new
But the grass grows up and covers,
Disappears, leaving the new thing
Underneath the old thing still,
No function but to have been.

What were their recipes for right?
Methods were endless, unendurable
Two ends of the log never rocked
And *points of percentage* sank
With the market, no gain
With leveraging averages there.

Only the bindings brightened,
Steady in their crimson, puce, green/blue.
Laid in on texts, laid out on
Inspissated answers,
No flowage from Parnassus.

BASICALLY BABY DESIGN

The trouble with Reason was it tried
too mindly to make it for everyone
to basically start look and jump on
certain goings on more or less
indifferent to the e.e.cummings
and so with basically baby design
more or bicycly less, it more or less
innocently walked thrill-ride forth
onto the choo-choo tracks of
The Last Train from La Guardia
with nothing on but its Justin boots
which were basically all that was left
and that ever since as they say
has pretty much been that.

EXPLAINING PAIN

The pain is never there,
Not where it seems to the pained
To be. It is some other, some
Unforeseen place like, perhaps
Or perhaps not, but a neuron
Or a nucleus or something
Else, somewhere else.
We doctors have proof of
What we say, this false
Presence of what is absent,
From history of pain-in-the-leg
Where there is no leg at all,
The entire leg off. All of it.
But a person still says "I feel pain!"
Right there where it's missing.

So the pain can't be where it's felt.
And the first and firmest relief
For what may be indicative
Of pain is to operate under
The sound, certain conviction
Of the pain's not being there
Where in vain one thinks it, but
Elsewhere, and thus you can
Understand what's otherwise
Impossible to understand
Without doctors to comfort
And explain (which is what
I am doing right now):

The uncharitable task I have
I do, unmasking—one might say—
The pain and pointing to its true
Location wherever if ever
It's found. Correctivity is all,
And the best relief ('til a better
One, if ever it's found, is found)
Is to treat what you think's a pain
With what you're certain's *not*—
A dog, for example, but *like* a dog
Anyway, when the dog is offending,
To *say* to the dog, *Down dog!*
And stay down! And if the dog
Stays *up*, whose fault is that!

WHEN WRITHING

When writhing of dourselves
We must bruise a whacky
l'Ongwitch to lunge with
In sumquat like
The contrastruction
Of a Goldberg Kartoum,
Or whither in hollow seminaries
Of abouted sense.

Blueness leds me
Be ceruse, as I'm
Heaving my heavingness
Debouching my bouts
Decanting my rants
From headshed to ragepage
With sediments to match.

No touch of sublimity's
Merchant of Venice.
But I can squeak
As swill as rathers
Would when I chew
'S or what gives a fit
To William Hazlitt
Who once was new
'S but now forgotten,
Who wrote "with fervor"
XXI valoriums.

(Ong, Walter J. a key
scholar in field of
Orality)

AN UNPRODUCTIVE DAY
WITH MY INTELLECT

Absolved from having to solve the first
By its self-contradictory nurture
I dissed same from misseration
Yawning widely behind my hand.
And

As the second and penultimate was already
Stuffed all together with excessivenesses
Altogether too similar to my own
No confusions could be drawn
Quartered, pureed or compacted
And

As I absolutely refused to compound
What was de facto already incredibly
I cast my asperities widely
With reinless feeling
Obesity, obesity, obesity.
And

Facing the finally sere and wasted so
No substance was to be seen or discovered
But a thin stalk of permeability and hype
Primitively weaving in the hot pale wind
I by then searching for a figurative firmness
Furtively mounted unflirtingly
As a man on a hipped horse
With glanders beside
But no bride And
And so to bed.

ON THE SELF AS SELF: FOUR VIEWS

I.
Who the here's content to be a self
Unamong the starry bangled
Going searching for it.
Who is there not already
Looking for a self-contempt
Content with the self he is?
What self is there anywhere
To content a self who's somewhere else?
Why doesn't everyone just stop
Stand and look around the mountains
For the Rockettes red glare.

II.
See the homeward paths
See the homeward binds
See the homeward bounds
And look elsewhere angelpuss.

III.

Familiar paths to marryland
The skirted boarded paths of nightly
See them root and germinal
Early before the Sun goes doom
And the going's gone of them
See the rowed selfs all in a line
And pick the very model of
A noble self of merchandise.

IV.

Want to be another self
To fit the same self's mirror?
A Sunday self with a home-
Body to boot? And Jesus
Wants you for a sunbeam.
Ask not what self could do
For JFK or Jesus, ask what
KFC can do to find a self,
Or go where everybody knows
To find a self is: why not try
Where you left your cell phone.

FOR THE YOU

I know of course for a certainly that you
(Others before) having samed the same feelings
That cannot but emphatically second,
Yes, my yes, third and fourth (like those
Sanphonies of Beethoven you know
Belize and Bartook) what all of us
Most want to see eventuate in
Happiness. In happiness for you!
For it's the *You* we all of us aim for
(Poets and program retinues, revenuers)
For the delving of reality and beingness
Over and above all be still and always
For the *You*, the vigorous deciduous
You disappearing in the brisk of winter
Emulsifying in the smooth Frost, or
Well-oiled orations of Spring—as we all
Love calling it (as you know, you knew
So well.) I do not matter but that you
Who do, Udo, (*vous perdu* do) who do
Matter, and matters of childlike
Concentrated self of who
You are you do: *matter*. But getting
Yonder, you see, beyond
Where you've stuck us, the we'res—
Oh can you see? Like Empartial
Clubmissions of Old. Or of older
Oldness and the decades after
Decay into wisdom they say; you too
Some once. So let us implore
The culturant optionts together,

Family-history-like, children so fueled
With hops, scotch; and people so nice are
To other people, but not so nice
As the *I*'s of us is to the *You's* of you,
The I's of us too with the *vous* of Yous:
And so a sing-song here is songed:

One some should noce
Sum some should care
None one or some one
Should not die, along die,
Die, die along with only
The *I* of the *You* of it.

You are in the arms of I and safe.
The I are the arms of (safe and around
(You)). be Life, be Vast, vast. as
Unclear the world as in the thing
To I. What I have not mentioned.

(Songed Thus. Thus the song.)

POEMS FOR AN AFTERNOON

1.   Dance round before rescue
    Place what you will
    Where you have it
    At frequencies no
    None of those
    That will behold
    But in some
    Wry system of
    juvenescence.

2.   There were those
    But others, too
    At angles often,
    Careless thus
    At odds, at enmity
    Annoyed
    No more was done;
    And they wore on
    Years then and space
    Foregoing ending
    Always unquiet
    Still unquiet.

3.   Like lace
    Fabric so fashioned
    To see into time
    Eyes ascending
    Treeless rise
    Nor nothing of pine
    Of spruce projecting
    Above the rim
    The curve of rind.

FRONT ROW

Several years ago
I sat in the front row
As all the strings in the orchestra
Hit the first fortissimo
Perpendicular arpeggio
Of Weber's Overture
To *Euryanthe*, feeling sure
Elation would carry
To the third balcony
Front row.
But then suppose
The rising song had stopped
Rows and rows before
Before the front row:
Terrorists
Even here?

LA VALSE

And forgive them their three-quarter time
The flood of sweetness within the gown
The crisp and swelling mirrored glide
Pulsing rising to innocent charm
Repeated chorus of climax subsiding.

Forgive them their body, their *Yes* of joy
Their unprovoked contradiction of all
That law's embarrassments hold true;
And forgive above all their own deeply held
Conviction of immortality.

WHY MARIANNE MOORE
IS THE FREEST POET

Because Miss Moore's "because" is
    always diaphanous
as though but some slight thread
    unsettled, was
floating by a world just stirring,
    blown by
from some distant action as yet
    unknown, knowable
but by the weight of a single
    thread
upon her wrist inviting, nay!
    demanding
ice tongs to fetch it up.

So much to be gathered
    so slowly in
refusing every impulse
    to identify, until
the weight of airlessness itself,
    itself was
through nomenclature clarified
    by no heretofore
machinery known. Only

    then, *because*.

THEN THE BOOKS

Then the books grew
and the books grew
and growing they
sometimes changed
and shrank, but
for the ever part
of present, of past,
the books grew and
volumes were added
to volumes and books
became more the same
sometimes and sometimes
the bindings meta-
morphosed into books
and the books grew.

And as they grew
we sometimes grew
along with them or
against, but grew,
but over and alive
all the books grew
displacing themselves
on the shelves or on
any flat places
and grew; stayed
or left but back
they came and they grew.

On shelves and in
the spaces they grew
and were weighty
sometimes as well
they said mightily,

and so they grew
and became both
new and old simul-
taneously growing,
held now sometimes

on new shelves in
sculpt places and
doors, light and with
glass gleamed before
and behind them,
the door with pleasant
chicks *clicks*
when they opened
or closed around
the books that still
grew, spreading
along to buildings
older often than some
of the books, gathering
places for the books
as they grew beyond
grounds, past measure,
where both took on
strange new old-smellings
of books and their en-
closures, support
not even as the books,
though, that grew
and grew out
from upon the shelves
and grew out from under
and beyond the eaves,
the shingles, thicker
than pages of books
as the books swelled

---

to match them,
and still the books grew
and from them plots
and places, and places
forgotten, and purposes
now no longer
understood.

Then darkness swelled
from under them
and spread and made
darkness, while the books
still grew and some
pleaded light.

And there were bindings
still upon them
around the pages
and of the thoughts
and news and what was
unencumbered, around.

And then
darkness and dense light
mingled and were thought
the same, and the bindings
and all was said
(didn't they say?
they said they'd say)
again said and mingled
and were told to say
what they meant
and mingled and
they said the same
as books. Bound
soft, some hard.

WINTRY SINGING—2003

" . . . the song is a varied warble, rendered as *liberty, liberty, liberty*"
North American Birdfeeder Handbook

High on a twisted country hill
Under a shrunken frigid sky
Framed by harvested amber grains
A Ruby-crowned kinglet sits.

He sings in thirty degrees of frost
Such a flickering pianissimo:

Am I hearing *liberty*, *liberty* . . . ?
I take it for genuine song, and I rush
Filling, overflowing the seed-tray.
"For the birds" is that now what they say?

WINTERING

Not for me has the dedication faded
with the swelling elsewheres of corpulent
mergers and outsourcing of compound
six percent interest in the social fabric.
My sensitive foot takes the measure
wherever a foot can be put down
I will put it, on price at the pump
in the mezzanine or the grocery cart.

And while some folks say *don't*—
don't we need more guns and gumshoes
more safety inspections of barbed wire
byways, borders, fields and routes of
escape and the flyways of currency
exchanges—say look at what's happened
to the networks of life, the trials
the fearings, the tears—so much hilarity
in need of being shed. But I don't say
listen to me. And I don't say take
your pulse frequently in the nervy
framework of your eloquent thoughts
of flushing from a timely foreclosure
as close as banked yesterday or
on the troubled expanse of
Wright's wronged prairies.

I would tell you if I could. But
haven't you a friend who winters,,,?
Tajikistan or the Dardanelles?

BROODING WITH BURCHFIELD *

* See *Heat Waves in a Swamp: The Paintings of Charles Burchfield*
Gober, Hammer Museum; 2010

•

"*Aimless Brooding* lurks in the scalloped shadows under the eaves . . ."

Brooding is not
a friendly word,
neither *Bakelite*
nor *abrogate* nor
aborigine or *Fitch*.

Recall of *Lear*
the *no, no, no, no*'s
so suddenly sodden,
a lachrymose affair.

Are there words solely
for landscape, as what
say *expansive*,
rampant, or dissolute?

Can objects be
so represented as to be
conventional both and
meaningless? Or
how deep before *sub-
liminal* is too labored
for commentary?

Please say "*Armory
Show*" to me
and I remember
a hotdog, so
sublimely grilled
there on a day
in 1934. Ah!
. . . Ah! . . . Ah!

Words are linearity
stretched for volume
as volume gas
swelling for weight,
converted to lace
draping age with
pale shade?

A Tree
in four seasons is
. . . well . . . Oh my!
A tree. Or . . . ?
up and
more solid than
soliloquy or
sigh?

Ideas
should be round
like fire, and what is
valued-virtue,
if not vivid as
color, *rejoice* as
smoke.

And I remember:
Was it Blake
Who had something
To say about
Gas . . . ?

SONG FOR A LOSER ONCE WHO WON

Suppose it's been forty-seven
years since they asked you—
weighing the filigree of your
delicate response
(an emulsified hesitancy
uncertainty and chagrin)
with more balance of their knowing
accurately shooting from hip and lip
the hop and dance of supreme
award and prejudged preference
post judged affirming of
near-best in class, masterly *dones*,
nonpareils since Dante did
Tolstoi and Mark Twain followed, or
the other way around: **would you**
(coming at last to the question)
waiting still in your virgin unknowing
at last find, (without apology
afterglow, honorableness or
appeal to still other persons
or processes authoritarian or
licensed) **and read the book?**
Cover to cover? And follow with
acknowledgments of country's
long-failed acknowledgments?

Or will you execute evermore excuse
in the dust of dreariness long settled
over the objects' movement from
shelf to shelf to make room for
altogether nuances of glory and
fame and *bests* since ever before
Shaxpere beat out Gavin Douglas
bishop of Dunkeld, third son of
Archibald fifth earl of Angus
(Em'y Dinglehouse was but not yet
been discovered) and all that was
frozen from cover to cover of
crisp yellowing matter were
spiders that suck their fill, agree?

Isn't it more possible than *maybe*
for fame to come too absolutely
late for one too unfortunately
soon for the other too indifferently
observed and too in good faith post-
poned while progress, circus,
popcorn and pomp rampantly
rolled and prevailed against
both the *Twelve Against the Gods*
and against the gods and justice?

How could you make it matter
more than with the small cash
howsoever minute you got (you gave
to the man who sold you the chair
you gave to the wife who fled with
the chair, took with her the house)
and this is now presently
your performance and recompense?

Complain therefore not, but
compose yourself yet, and strike
still anew into the glossary of
life's everlasting nugatoriness
of what's at best dilatory as well
as sequelless in the altogether.
Aftermath comes calculus
with its countless quadrilles
inflations and diapasons
lusty disfiguring, ill-disguised all.

Sleep on it. Sleep. Step
    Step on it. Sleep.

CREDO

· · · · · · · · · · · · · · · · ·

WE BELIEVE

Our purpose as a nation requires unity and
Our purpose as a Unity requires diversity
We must divest ourselves in turn of some diversity
To ensure that power will be sufficiently unified
To have an effect when and wherever
Purpose is expected or desired.

Citizens will carry out their legacy of service
But will not be troubled to remember
Everything our mandatory service calls for
Only the much of a good passing grade
On a broad spectrum of tests to ensure
Our facility when contemplating the ends
To which all purpose of a meaningful kind
Is to be enacted, maintained and glorified
With certain obvious and colorful reminders
Of the rightness and proper application of
The glorification. Of the legacy. Of service.

Everyone's ideals shall be freely expressed
And valued according to their reflection
Of commitments to the honor of the whole
In the service of steadfast applicability
To Our universal vibrancy.

Freedom for all is for all and therefore
Undisruptable by individualization.
And losable, deniable, and destructible
Only on specification measures
Religiously examined as to revelation
Of their genesis, exodus, and fundability
Nor to such means is any appeal seekable
Or entertained, as containment of the balance
Of freedom is never less than it was.
Our purpose will be served.

Printed in the United States
By Bookmasters